Dear Lord, Hear My Prayer...

Prayer Request Notebook

Wendy Ball Bridgeman

Dear Lord, Hear My Prayer...

Prayer Request Notebook

Scripture quotations taken from The Holy Bible, New International Version NIV
Copyright 1973, 1978, 1984, 2011 by Biblica, INC.
Used by permission. All Rights reserved worldwide

ISBN: 978-1-7349862-6-6

Dedicated to Rorey, Kennedi and Myles....thank you for all of your love and support.
I Love You!

Introduction

If you're like me, you have every good intention of praying for someone. If you're really like me, sometimes, you forget. This notebook was created for just this reason; to help us remember those we'd like to uplift in prayer. It's rarely a short list, so it's not surprising we can struggle some days.

This notebook provides a space to list those you wish to pray for, that might slip your mind—but never your heart. As well as, a space to write your own personal prayers.

You will always be able to go back and read your answered prayers and reflect on the many blessings in life; both large and small.

And above all else, remember that He is listening.

My prayer is that you will find this notebook useful and it will increase your prayer life.

"Our Father in heaven, hallowed be your name, your kingdom come, your will be done, on earth as it is in heaven. Give us today our daily bread. And forgive us our debts, as we also have forgiven our debtors. And lead us not into temptation, but deliver us from the evil one." Amen

"Dear Lord,

Date: _____

My Prayer Request...

_____

_____

_____

_____

_____

_____

_____

_____

_____

_____

_____

_____

_____

_____

_____

_____

_____

_____

_____

_____

_____

_____

Hear My Prayer"

Prayer Request For Others...

_____

_____

_____

_____

_____

_____

_____

_____

_____

_____

_____

_____

<u>Answered Prayers</u>

_____

_____

_____

_____

_____

"Dear Lord,

Date: _____

My Prayer Request...

_____

_____

_____

_____

_____

_____

_____

_____

_____

_____

_____

_____

_____

_____

_____

_____

_____

_____

_____

_____

_____

Hear My Prayer"

Prayer Request For Others...

_____

_____

_____

_____

_____

_____

_____

_____

_____

_____

_____

_____

_____

_____

Answered Prayers

_____

_____

_____

_____

_____

"Dear Lord,

Date: _____

My Prayer Request...

_____

_____

_____

_____

_____

_____

_____

_____

_____

_____

_____

_____

_____

_____

_____

_____

_____

_____

_____

_____

_____

Hear My Prayer"

Prayer Request For Others...

_____

_____

_____

_____

_____

_____

_____

_____

_____

_____

_____

_____

Answered Prayers

_____

_____

_____

_____

_____

"Dear Lord,

Date: _____

My Prayer Request...

_____

_____

_____

_____

_____

_____

_____

_____

_____

_____

_____

_____

_____

_____

_____

_____

_____

_____

_____

_____

_____

Hear My Prayer"

Prayer Request For Others...

_____

_____

_____

_____

_____

_____

_____

_____

_____

_____

_____

_____

Answered Prayers

_____

_____

_____

_____

_____

"Dear Lord,

Date: _____

My Prayer Request...

_____

_____

_____

_____

_____

_____

_____

_____

_____

_____

_____

_____

_____

_____

_____

_____

_____

_____

_____

_____

_____

Hear My Prayer"

Prayer Request For Others...

_____

_____

_____

_____

_____

_____

_____

_____

_____

_____

_____

_____

Answered Prayers

_____

_____

_____

_____

_____

_____

"Dear Lord,

Date: _____

My Prayer Request...

_____

_____

_____

_____

_____

_____

_____

_____

_____

_____

_____

_____

_____

_____

_____

_____

_____

_____

_____

_____

_____

Hear My Prayer"

Prayer Request For Others...

_____

_____

_____

_____

_____

_____

_____

_____

_____

_____

_____

_____

Answered Prayers

_____

_____

_____

_____

_____

_____

"Dear Lord,

Date: _____

My Prayer Request...

_____

_____

_____

_____

_____

_____

_____

_____

_____

_____

_____

_____

_____

_____

_____

_____

_____

_____

_____

_____

_____

_____

Hear My Prayer"

Prayer Request For Others...

_____

_____

_____

_____

_____

_____

_____

_____

_____

_____

_____

_____

<u>Answered Prayers</u>

_____

_____

_____

_____

_____

"He will respond to the prayer of the destitute; he will not despise their plea."

Psalm 102:17

"Dear Lord,

Date: _____

My Prayer Request...

_____

_____

_____

_____

_____

_____

_____

_____

_____

_____

_____

_____

_____

_____

_____

_____

_____

_____

_____

_____

_____

_____

_____

Hear My Prayer"

Prayer Request For Others...

_____

_____

_____

_____

_____

_____

_____

_____

_____

_____

_____

_____

_____

Answered Prayers

_____

_____

_____

_____

_____

"Dear Lord,

Date: _____

My Prayer Request...

_____

_____

_____

_____

_____

_____

_____

_____

_____

_____

_____

_____

_____

_____

_____

_____

_____

_____

_____

_____

_____

_____

Hear My Prayer"

Prayer Request For Others...

_____

_____

_____

_____

_____

_____

_____

_____

_____

_____

_____

_____

Answered Prayers

_____

_____

_____

_____

_____

"Dear Lord,

Date: _____

My Prayer Request...

_____
_____
_____
_____
_____
_____
_____
_____
_____
_____
_____
_____
_____
_____
_____
_____
_____
_____
_____
_____
_____
_____
_____
_____

Hear My Prayer"

Prayer Request For Others...

_____
_____
_____
_____
_____
_____
_____
_____
_____
_____
_____
_____
_____

Answered Prayers

_____
_____
_____
_____
_____

"Dear Lord,

Date: _____

My Prayer Request...

_____

_____

_____

_____

_____

_____

_____

_____

_____

_____

_____

_____

_____

_____

_____

_____

_____

_____

_____

_____

_____

_____

_____

Hear My Prayer"

Prayer Request For Others...

_____

_____

_____

_____

_____

_____

_____

_____

_____

_____

_____

_____

<u>Answered Prayers</u>

_____

_____

_____

_____

_____

"Dear Lord,

Date: _____

My Prayer Request...

_____

_____

_____

_____

_____

_____

_____

_____

_____

_____

_____

_____

_____

_____

_____

_____

_____

_____

_____

_____

Hear My Prayer"

Prayer Request For Others...

_____

_____

_____

_____

_____

_____

_____

_____

_____

_____

_____

_____

_____

<u>Answered Prayers</u>

_____

_____

_____

_____

_____

"Dear Lord,

Date: _____

My Prayer Request...

_____

_____

_____

_____

_____

_____

_____

_____

_____

_____

_____

_____

_____

_____

_____

_____

_____

_____

_____

_____

_____

_____

Hear My Prayer"

Prayer Request For Others...

_____
_____
_____
_____
_____
_____
_____
_____
_____
_____
_____
_____
_____

Answered Prayers

_____
_____
_____
_____
_____

"Dear Lord,

Date: _____

My Prayer Request...

_____

_____

_____

_____

_____

_____

_____

_____

_____

_____

_____

_____

_____

_____

_____

_____

_____

_____

_____

_____

_____

_____

Hear My Prayer"

Prayer Request For Others...

_____

_____

_____

_____

_____

_____

_____

_____

_____

_____

_____

_____

Answered Prayers

_____

_____

_____

_____

_____

For the eyes of the Lord are on the righteous and his ears are attentive to their prayer, but the face of the Lord is against those who do evil."

1 Peter 3:12

"Dear Lord,

Date: _____

My Prayer Request...

_____

_____

_____

_____

_____

_____

_____

_____

_____

_____

_____

_____

_____

_____

_____

_____

_____

_____

_____

_____

_____

Hear My Prayer"

Prayer Request For Others...

_____

_____

_____

_____

_____

_____

_____

_____

_____

_____

_____

_____

_____

_____

Answered Prayers

_____

_____

_____

_____

_____

_____

"Dear Lord,

Date: _____

My Prayer Request...

_____

_____

_____

_____

_____

_____

_____

_____

_____

_____

_____

_____

_____

_____

_____

_____

_____

_____

_____

_____

_____

Hear My Prayer"

Prayer Request For Others...

_____

_____

_____

_____

_____

_____

_____

_____

_____

_____

_____

_____

Answered Prayers

_____

_____

_____

_____

_____

_____

"Dear Lord,

Date: _____

My Prayer Request...

_____

_____

_____

_____

_____

_____

_____

_____

_____

_____

_____

_____

_____

_____

_____

_____

_____

_____

_____

_____

_____

_____

Hear My Prayer"

Prayer Request For Others...

_____

_____

_____

_____

_____

_____

_____

_____

_____

_____

_____

_____

Answered Prayers

_____

_____

_____

_____

_____

"Dear Lord,

Date: _____

My Prayer Request...

_____

_____

_____

_____

_____

_____

_____

_____

_____

_____

_____

_____

_____

_____

_____

_____

_____

_____

_____

_____

_____

_____

Hear My Prayer"

Prayer Request For Others...

_____

_____

_____

_____

_____

_____

_____

_____

_____

_____

_____

<u>Answered Prayers</u>

_____

_____

_____

_____

_____

"Dear Lord,

Date: _____

My Prayer Request...

_____

_____

_____

_____

_____

_____

_____

_____

_____

_____

_____

_____

_____

_____

_____

_____

_____

_____

_____

_____

_____

_____

Hear My Prayer"

Prayer Request For Others...

_____

_____

_____

_____

_____

_____

_____

_____

_____

_____

_____

_____

_____

<u>Answered Prayers</u>

_____

_____

_____

_____

_____

"Dear Lord,

Date: _____

My Prayer Request...

_____

_____

_____

_____

_____

_____

_____

_____

_____

_____

_____

_____

_____

_____

_____

_____

_____

_____

_____

_____

_____

Hear My Prayer"

Prayer Request For Others...

_____

_____

_____

_____

_____

_____

_____

_____

_____

_____

_____

<u>Answered Prayers</u>

_____

_____

_____

_____

_____

"Dear Lord,

Date: _____

My Prayer Request...

_____
_____
_____
_____
_____
_____
_____
_____
_____
_____
_____
_____
_____
_____
_____
_____
_____
_____
_____
_____
_____
_____

Hear My Prayer"

Prayer Request For Others...

_____

_____

_____

_____

_____

_____

_____

_____

_____

_____

_____

_____

Answered Prayers

_____

_____

_____

_____

_____

"You will pray to him, and he will hear you, and you will fulfill your vows."

Job 22:27

"Dear Lord,

Date: _____

My Prayer Request...

_____

_____

_____

_____

_____

_____

_____

_____

_____

_____

_____

_____

_____

_____

_____

_____

_____

_____

_____

_____

_____

_____

Hear My Prayer"

Prayer Request For Others...

_____

_____

_____

_____

_____

_____

_____

_____

_____

_____

_____

_____

Answered Prayers

_____

_____

_____

_____

_____

_____

"Dear Lord,

Date: _____

My Prayer Request...

_____

_____

_____

_____

_____

_____

_____

_____

_____

_____

_____

_____

_____

_____

_____

_____

_____

_____

_____

_____

_____

_____

Hear My Prayer"

Prayer Request For Others...

_____

_____

_____

_____

_____

_____

_____

_____

_____

_____

_____

_____

Answered Prayers

_____

_____

_____

_____

_____

_____

"Dear Lord,

Date: _____

My Prayer Request...

_____

_____

_____

_____

_____

_____

_____

_____

_____

_____

_____

_____

_____

_____

_____

_____

_____

_____

_____

_____

_____

_____

Hear My Prayer"

Prayer Request For Others...

_____

_____

_____

_____

_____

_____

_____

_____

_____

_____

_____

_____

_____

<u>Answered Prayers</u>

_____

_____

_____

_____

_____

"Dear Lord,

Date: _____

My Prayer Request...

_____

_____

_____

_____

_____

_____

_____

_____

_____

_____

_____

_____

_____

_____

_____

_____

_____

_____

_____

_____

_____

Hear My Prayer"

Prayer Request For Others...

_____

_____

_____

_____

_____

_____

_____

_____

_____

_____

_____

_____

Answered Prayers

_____

_____

_____

_____

_____

"Dear Lord,

Date: _____

My Prayer Request...

_____

_____

_____

_____

_____

_____

_____

_____

_____

_____

_____

_____

_____

_____

_____

_____

_____

_____

_____

_____

_____

_____

_____

Hear My Prayer"

Prayer Request For Others...

_____

_____

_____

_____

_____

_____

_____

_____

_____

_____

_____

_____

_____

<u>Answered Prayers</u>

_____

_____

_____

_____

_____

_____

"Dear Lord,

Date: _____

My Prayer Request...

_____

_____

_____

_____

_____

_____

_____

_____

_____

_____

_____

_____

_____

_____

_____

_____

_____

_____

_____

Hear My Prayer"

Prayer Request For Others...

_____

_____

_____

_____

_____

_____

_____

_____

_____

_____

_____

_____

_____

Answered Prayers

_____

_____

_____

_____

_____

"Dear Lord,

Date: _____

My Prayer Request...

_____

_____

_____

_____

_____

_____

_____

_____

_____

_____

_____

_____

_____

_____

_____

_____

_____

_____

_____

_____

_____

_____

_____

Hear My Prayer"

Prayer Request For Others...

_____

_____

_____

_____

_____

_____

_____

_____

_____

_____

_____

_____

Answered Prayers

_____

_____

_____

_____

_____

"The Lord is far from the wicked, but he hears the prayer of the righteous."

Proverbs 15:29

"Dear Lord,

Date: _____

My Prayer Request...

_____

_____

_____

_____

_____

_____

_____

_____

_____

_____

_____

_____

_____

_____

_____

_____

_____

_____

_____

_____

_____

_____

Hear My Prayer"

Prayer Request For Others...

_____
_____
_____
_____
_____
_____
_____
_____
_____
_____
_____
_____
_____

Answered Prayers

_____
_____
_____
_____
_____

"Dear Lord,

Date: _____

My Prayer Request...

_____

_____

_____

_____

_____

_____

_____

_____

_____

_____

_____

_____

_____

_____

_____

_____

_____

_____

_____

_____

_____

_____

_____

Hear My Prayer"

Prayer Request For Others...

_____

_____

_____

_____

_____

_____

_____

_____

_____

_____

_____

_____

Answered Prayers

_____

_____

_____

_____

_____

"Dear Lord,

Date: _____

My Prayer Request...

_____

_____

_____

_____

_____

_____

_____

_____

_____

_____

_____

_____

_____

_____

_____

_____

_____

_____

_____

_____

_____

_____

_____

_____

Hear My Prayer"

Prayer Request For Others...

_____

_____

_____

_____

_____

_____

_____

_____

_____

_____

_____

_____

_____

<u>Answered Prayers</u>

_____

_____

_____

_____

_____

"Dear Lord,

Date: _____

My Prayer Request...

_____

_____

_____

_____

_____

_____

_____

_____

_____

_____

_____

_____

_____

_____

_____

_____

_____

_____

_____

_____

Hear My Prayer"

Prayer Request For Others...

_____

_____

_____

_____

_____

_____

_____

_____

_____

_____

_____

_____

Answered Prayers

_____

_____

_____

_____

_____

"Dear Lord,

Date: _____

My Prayer Request...

_____

_____

_____

_____

_____

_____

_____

_____

_____

_____

_____

_____

_____

_____

_____

_____

_____

_____

_____

_____

_____

_____

Hear My Prayer"

Prayer Request For Others...

_____

_____

_____

_____

_____

_____

_____

_____

_____

_____

_____

_____

Answered Prayers

_____

_____

_____

_____

_____

_____

"Dear Lord,

Date: _____

My Prayer Request...

_____

_____

_____

_____

_____

_____

_____

_____

_____

_____

_____

_____

_____

_____

_____

_____

_____

_____

_____

_____

_____

_____

_____

Hear My Prayer"

Prayer Request For Others...

_____

_____

_____

_____

_____

_____

_____

_____

_____

_____

_____

_____

_____

<u>Answered Prayers</u>

_____

_____

_____

_____

_____

"Dear Lord,

Date: _____

My Prayer Request...

_____

_____

_____

_____

_____

_____

_____

_____

_____

_____

_____

_____

_____

_____

_____

_____

_____

_____

_____

_____

_____

Hear My Prayer"

Prayer Request For Others...

_____

_____

_____

_____

_____

_____

_____

_____

_____

_____

_____

_____

Answered Prayers

_____

_____

_____

_____

_____

_____

"Devote yourselves to prayer, being watchful and thankful."

Colossians 4:2

"Dear Lord,

Date: _____

My Prayer Request...

_____

_____

_____

_____

_____

_____

_____

_____

_____

_____

_____

_____

_____

_____

_____

_____

_____

_____

_____

_____

Hear My Prayer"

Prayer Request For Others...

_____

_____

_____

_____

_____

_____

_____

_____

_____

_____

_____

_____

<u>Answered Prayers</u>

_____

_____

_____

_____

_____

"Dear Lord,

Date: _____

My Prayer Request...

_____

_____

_____

_____

_____

_____

_____

_____

_____

_____

_____

_____

_____

_____

_____

_____

_____

_____

_____

_____

_____

_____

Hear My Prayer"

Prayer Request For Others...

_____
_____
_____
_____
_____
_____
_____
_____
_____
_____
_____
_____
_____

<u>Answered Prayers</u>

_____
_____
_____
_____
_____

"Dear Lord,

Date: _____

My Prayer Request...

_____

_____

_____

_____

_____

_____

_____

_____

_____

_____

_____

_____

_____

_____

_____

_____

_____

_____

_____

_____

Hear My Prayer"

Prayer Request For Others...

_____

_____

_____

_____

_____

_____

_____

_____

_____

_____

_____

_____

Answered Prayers

_____

_____

_____

_____

_____

_____

"Dear Lord,

Date: _____

My Prayer Request...

_____

_____

_____

_____

_____

_____

_____

_____

_____

_____

_____

_____

_____

_____

_____

_____

_____

_____

_____

_____

_____

_____

Hear My Prayer"

Prayer Request For Others...

_____

_____

_____

_____

_____

_____

_____

_____

_____

_____

_____

_____

Answered Prayers

_____

_____

_____

_____

_____

"Dear Lord,

Date: _____

My Prayer Request...

_____

_____

_____

_____

_____

_____

_____

_____

_____

_____

_____

_____

_____

_____

_____

_____

_____

_____

_____

_____

_____

_____

Hear My Prayer"

Prayer Request For Others...

_____
_____
_____
_____
_____
_____
_____
_____
_____
_____
_____
_____
_____

Answered Prayers

_____
_____
_____
_____
_____
_____

"Dear Lord,

Date: _____

My Prayer Request...

_____

_____

_____

_____

_____

_____

_____

_____

_____

_____

_____

_____

_____

_____

_____

_____

_____

_____

_____

_____

Hear My Prayer"

Prayer Request For Others...

_____

_____

_____

_____

_____

_____

_____

_____

_____

_____

_____

_____

Answered Prayers

_____

_____

_____

_____

_____

"Dear Lord,

Date: _____

My Prayer Request...

_____

_____

_____

_____

_____

_____

_____

_____

_____

_____

_____

_____

_____

_____

_____

_____

_____

_____

_____

_____

_____

_____

Hear My Prayer"

Prayer Request For Others...

_____

_____

_____

_____

_____

_____

_____

_____

_____

_____

_____

_____

<u>Answered Prayers</u>

_____

_____

_____

_____

_____

_____

"Do not be anxious about anything, but in every situation, by prayer and petition, with thanksgiving, present your requests to God."

Philippians 4:6

"Dear Lord,

Date: _____

My Prayer Request...

_____

_____

_____

_____

_____

_____

_____

_____

_____

_____

_____

_____

_____

_____

_____

_____

_____

_____

_____

_____

_____

_____

_____

_____

Hear My Prayer"

Prayer Request For Others...

_____

_____

_____

_____

_____

_____

_____

_____

_____

_____

_____

_____

_____

<u>Answered Prayers</u>

_____

_____

_____

_____

_____

_____

"Dear Lord,

Date: _____

My Prayer Request...

_____

_____

_____

_____

_____

_____

_____

_____

_____

_____

_____

_____

_____

_____

_____

_____

_____

_____

_____

_____

Hear My Prayer"

Prayer Request For Others...

_____

_____

_____

_____

_____

_____

_____

_____

_____

_____

_____

_____

_____

Answered Prayers

_____

_____

_____

_____

_____

"Dear Lord,

Date: _____

My Prayer Request...

_____

_____

_____

_____

_____

_____

_____

_____

_____

_____

_____

_____

_____

_____

_____

_____

_____

_____

_____

Hear My Prayer"

Prayer Request For Others...

_____

_____

_____

_____

_____

_____

_____

_____

_____

_____

_____

_____

Answered Prayers

_____

_____

_____

_____

_____

_____

"Dear Lord,

Date: _____

My Prayer Request...

_____

_____

_____

_____

_____

_____

_____

_____

_____

_____

_____

_____

_____

_____

_____

_____

_____

_____

_____

_____

_____

Hear My Prayer"

Prayer Request For Others...

_____

_____

_____

_____

_____

_____

_____

_____

_____

_____

_____

_____

<u>Answered Prayers</u>

_____

_____

_____

_____

_____

"Dear Lord,

Date: _____

My Prayer Request...

_____

_____

_____

_____

_____

_____

_____

_____

_____

_____

_____

_____

_____

_____

_____

_____

_____

_____

_____

_____

_____

_____

Hear My Prayer"

Prayer Request For Others...

_____

_____

_____

_____

_____

_____

_____

_____

_____

_____

_____

_____

_____

Answered Prayers

_____

_____

_____

_____

_____

_____

"Dear Lord,

Date: _____

My Prayer Request...

_____

_____

_____

_____

_____

_____

_____

_____

_____

_____

_____

_____

_____

_____

_____

_____

_____

_____

_____

_____

_____

_____

Hear My Prayer"

Prayer Request For Others...

_____

_____

_____

_____

_____

_____

_____

_____

_____

_____

_____

_____

_____

<u>Answered Prayers</u>

_____

_____

_____

_____

_____

_____

"Dear Lord,

Date: _____

My Prayer Request...

_____

_____

_____

_____

_____

_____

_____

_____

_____

_____

_____

_____

_____

_____

_____

_____

_____

_____

_____

_____

_____

Hear My Prayer"

Prayer Request For Others...

_____

_____

_____

_____

_____

_____

_____

_____

_____

_____

_____

_____

<u>Answered Prayers</u>

_____

_____

_____

_____

_____

_____

"Hear my prayer, Lord; let my cry for help come to you."

Psalm 102:1

"Dear Lord,

Date: _____

My Prayer Request...

_____

_____

_____

_____

_____

_____

_____

_____

_____

_____

_____

_____

_____

_____

_____

_____

_____

_____

_____

_____

_____

_____

Hear My Prayer"

Prayer Request For Others...

_____

_____

_____

_____

_____

_____

_____

_____

_____

_____

_____

_____

Answered Prayers

_____

_____

_____

_____

_____

"Dear Lord,

Date: _____

My Prayer Request...

_____

_____

_____

_____

_____

_____

_____

_____

_____

_____

_____

_____

_____

_____

_____

_____

_____

_____

_____

_____

_____

_____

Hear My Prayer"

Prayer Request For Others...

_____

_____

_____

_____

_____

_____

_____

_____

_____

_____

_____

_____

<u>Answered Prayers</u>

_____

_____

_____

_____

_____

"Dear Lord,

Date: _____

My Prayer Request...

_____
_____
_____
_____
_____
_____
_____
_____
_____
_____
_____
_____
_____
_____
_____
_____
_____
_____
_____
_____
_____
_____
_____

Hear My Prayer"

Prayer Request For Others...

_____

_____

_____

_____

_____

_____

_____

_____

_____

_____

_____

_____

Answered Prayers

_____

_____

_____

_____

_____

"Dear Lord,

Date: _____

My Prayer Request...

_____

_____

_____

_____

_____

_____

_____

_____

_____

_____

_____

_____

_____

_____

_____

_____

_____

_____

_____

_____

_____

_____

_____

Hear My Prayer"

Prayer Request For Others...

_____

_____

_____

_____

_____

_____

_____

_____

_____

_____

_____

_____

_____

_____

_____

<u>Answered Prayers</u>

_____

_____

_____

_____

_____

_____

"Dear Lord,

Date: _____

My Prayer Request...

_____

_____

_____

_____

_____

_____

_____

_____

_____

_____

_____

_____

_____

_____

_____

_____

_____

_____

_____

_____

_____

_____

Hear My Prayer"

Prayer Request For Others...

_____

_____

_____

_____

_____

_____

_____

_____

_____

_____

_____

_____

<u>Answered Prayers</u>

_____

_____

_____

_____

_____

_____

"Dear Lord,

Date: _____

My Prayer Request...

_____

_____

_____

_____

_____

_____

_____

_____

_____

_____

_____

_____

_____

_____

_____

_____

_____

_____

_____

_____

Hear My Prayer"

Prayer Request For Others...

_____

_____

_____

_____

_____

_____

_____

_____

_____

_____

_____

_____

<u>Answered Prayers</u>

_____

_____

_____

_____

_____

_____

"Dear Lord,

Date: _____

My Prayer Request...

_____

_____

_____

_____

_____

_____

_____

_____

_____

_____

_____

_____

_____

_____

_____

_____

_____

_____

_____

_____

_____

Hear My Prayer"

Prayer Request For Others...

_____
_____
_____
_____
_____
_____
_____
_____
_____
_____
_____
_____
_____

<u>Answered Prayers</u>

_____
_____
_____
_____
_____

"The prayer of a righteous person is powerful and effective."

James 5:16

"Dear Lord,

Date: _____

My Prayer Request...

_____

_____

_____

_____

_____

_____

_____

_____

_____

_____

_____

_____

_____

_____

_____

_____

_____

_____

_____

_____

_____

Hear My Prayer"

Prayer Request For Others...

_____

_____

_____

_____

_____

_____

_____

_____

_____

_____

_____

_____

<u>Answered Prayers</u>

_____

_____

_____

_____

_____

"Dear Lord,

Date: _____

My Prayer Request...

_____

_____

_____

_____

_____

_____

_____

_____

_____

_____

_____

_____

_____

_____

_____

_____

_____

_____

_____

_____

_____

Hear My Prayer"

Prayer Request For Others...

_____
_____
_____
_____
_____
_____
_____
_____
_____
_____
_____
_____
_____

Answered Prayers

_____
_____
_____
_____
_____
_____

"Dear Lord,

Date: _____

My Prayer Request...

_____

_____

_____

_____

_____

_____

_____

_____

_____

_____

_____

_____

_____

_____

_____

_____

_____

_____

_____

_____

_____

_____

Hear My Prayer"

Prayer Request For Others...

_____

_____

_____

_____

_____

_____

_____

_____

_____

_____

_____

_____

Answered Prayers

_____

_____

_____

_____

_____

"Dear Lord,

Date: _____

My Prayer Request...

_____

_____

_____

_____

_____

_____

_____

_____

_____

_____

_____

_____

_____

_____

_____

_____

_____

_____

_____

_____

_____

Hear My Prayer"

Prayer Request For Others...

_____

_____

_____

_____

_____

_____

_____

_____

_____

_____

_____

<u>Answered Prayers</u>

_____

_____

_____

_____

_____

_____

"Dear Lord,

Date: _____

My Prayer Request...

_____

_____

_____

_____

_____

_____

_____

_____

_____

_____

_____

_____

_____

_____

_____

_____

_____

_____

_____

_____

_____

_____

_____

Hear My Prayer"

Prayer Request For Others...

_____

_____

_____

_____

_____

_____

_____

_____

_____

_____

_____

_____

_____

Answered Prayers

_____

_____

_____

_____

_____

"Dear Lord,

Date: _____

My Prayer Request...

_____

_____

_____

_____

_____

_____

_____

_____

_____

_____

_____

_____

_____

_____

_____

_____

_____

_____

_____

_____

_____

Hear My Prayer"

Prayer Request For Others...

_____

_____

_____

_____

_____

_____

_____

_____

_____

_____

_____

_____

_____

<u>Answered Prayers</u>

_____

_____

_____

_____

_____

"Dear Lord,

Date: _____

My Prayer Request...

_____

_____

_____

_____

_____

_____

_____

_____

_____

_____

_____

_____

_____

_____

_____

_____

_____

_____

_____

_____

_____

_____

_____

Hear My Prayer"

Prayer Request For Others...

_____

_____

_____

_____

_____

_____

_____

_____

_____

_____

_____

_____

<u>Answered Prayers</u>

_____

_____

_____

_____

_____

_____

"Then you will call on me and come and pray to me, and I will listen to you."

Jeremiah 29:12

"Dear Lord,

Date: _____

My Prayer Request...

_____

_____

_____

_____

_____

_____

_____

_____

_____

_____

_____

_____

_____

_____

_____

_____

_____

_____

_____

_____

Hear My Prayer"

Prayer Request For Others...

_____

_____

_____

_____

_____

_____

_____

_____

_____

_____

_____

_____

_____

_____

<u>Answered Prayers</u>

_____

_____

_____

_____

_____

"Dear Lord,

Date: _____

My Prayer Request...

_____

_____

_____

_____

_____

_____

_____

_____

_____

_____

_____

_____

_____

_____

_____

_____

_____

_____

_____

_____

_____

_____

Hear My Prayer"

Prayer Request For Others...

_____

_____

_____

_____

_____

_____

_____

_____

_____

_____

_____

_____

Answered Prayers

_____

_____

_____

_____

_____

"Dear Lord,

Date: _____

My Prayer Request...

_____

_____

_____

_____

_____

_____

_____

_____

_____

_____

_____

_____

_____

_____

_____

_____

_____

_____

_____

_____

_____

_____

Hear My Prayer"

Prayer Request For Others...

_____

_____

_____

_____

_____

_____

_____

_____

_____

_____

_____

_____

Answered Prayers

_____

_____

_____

_____

_____

"Dear Lord,

Date: _____

My Prayer Request...

_____

_____

_____

_____

_____

_____

_____

_____

_____

_____

_____

_____

_____

_____

_____

_____

_____

_____

_____

_____

_____

_____

_____

_____

_____

Hear My Prayer"

Prayer Request For Others...

_____

_____

_____

_____

_____

_____

_____

_____

_____

_____

_____

_____

Answered Prayers

_____

_____

_____

_____

_____

"Dear Lord,

Date: _____

My Prayer Request...

_____

_____

_____

_____

_____

_____

_____

_____

_____

_____

_____

_____

_____

_____

_____

_____

_____

_____

_____

_____

Hear My Prayer"

Prayer Request For Others...

_____
_____
_____
_____
_____
_____
_____
_____
_____
_____
_____
_____
_____

Answered Prayers

_____
_____
_____
_____
_____
_____

"Dear Lord,

Date: _____

My Prayer Request...

_____

_____

_____

_____

_____

_____

_____

_____

_____

_____

_____

_____

_____

_____

_____

_____

_____

_____

_____

_____

_____

_____

_____

Hear My Prayer"

Prayer Request For Others...

_____

_____

_____

_____

_____

_____

_____

_____

_____

_____

_____

_____

Answered Prayers

_____

_____

_____

_____

_____

_____

"Dear Lord,

Date: _____

My Prayer Request...

_____

_____

_____

_____

_____

_____

_____

_____

_____

_____

_____

_____

_____

_____

_____

_____

_____

_____

_____

_____

_____

_____

_____

Hear My Prayer"

Prayer Request For Others...

_____

_____

_____

_____

_____

_____

_____

_____

_____

_____

_____

_____

<u>Answered Prayers</u>

_____

_____

_____

_____

_____

_____

"Be joyful in hope, patient in affliction, faithful in prayer."

Romans 12:12

"Dear Lord,

Date: _____

My Prayer Request...

_____

_____

_____

_____

_____

_____

_____

_____

_____

_____

_____

_____

_____

_____

_____

_____

_____

_____

_____

_____

Hear My Prayer"

Prayer Request For Others...

_____

_____

_____

_____

_____

_____

_____

_____

_____

_____

_____

_____

_____

<u>Answered Prayers</u>

_____

_____

_____

_____

_____

_____

"Dear Lord,

Date: _____

My Prayer Request...

_____

_____

_____

_____

_____

_____

_____

_____

_____

_____

_____

_____

_____

_____

_____

_____

_____

_____

_____

_____

_____

_____

_____

_____

Hear My Prayer"

Prayer Request For Others...

_____

_____

_____

_____

_____

_____

_____

_____

_____

_____

_____

_____

Answered Prayers

_____

_____

_____

_____

_____

"Dear Lord,

Date: _____

My Prayer Request...

_____

_____

_____

_____

_____

_____

_____

_____

_____

_____

_____

_____

_____

_____

_____

_____

_____

_____

_____

_____

_____

Hear My Prayer"

Prayer Request For Others...

_____

_____

_____

_____

_____

_____

_____

_____

_____

_____

_____

_____

_____

<u>Answered Prayers</u>

_____

_____

_____

_____

_____

"Dear Lord,

Date: _____

My Prayer Request...

_____

_____

_____

_____

_____

_____

_____

_____

_____

_____

_____

_____

_____

_____

_____

_____

_____

_____

_____

_____

Hear My Prayer"

Prayer Request For Others...

_____
_____
_____
_____
_____
_____
_____
_____
_____
_____
_____
_____

Answered Prayers

_____
_____
_____
_____
_____

"Dear Lord,

Date: _____

My Prayer Request...

_____

_____

_____

_____

_____

_____

_____

_____

_____

_____

_____

_____

_____

_____

_____

_____

_____

_____

_____

_____

_____

_____

_____

_____

_____

Hear My Prayer"

Prayer Request For Others...

_____

_____

_____

_____

_____

_____

_____

_____

_____

_____

_____

_____

Answered Prayers

_____

_____

_____

_____

_____

"Dear Lord,

Date: _____

My Prayer Request...

_____

_____

_____

_____

_____

_____

_____

_____

_____

_____

_____

_____

_____

_____

_____

_____

_____

_____

_____

_____

_____

_____

Hear My Prayer"

Prayer Request For Others...

_____

_____

_____

_____

_____

_____

_____

_____

_____

_____

_____

_____

_____

<u>Answered Prayers</u>

_____

_____

_____

_____

_____

"Dear Lord,

Date: _____

My Prayer Request...

_____

_____

_____

_____

_____

_____

_____

_____

_____

_____

_____

_____

_____

_____

_____

_____

_____

_____

_____

_____

_____

_____

Hear My Prayer"

Prayer Request For Others...

_____

_____

_____

_____

_____

_____

_____

_____

_____

_____

_____

_____

_____

Answered Prayers

_____

_____

_____

_____

_____

"Therefore I tell you, whatever you ask for in prayer, believe that you have received it, and it will be yours."

Mark 11:24

"Dear Lord,

Date: _____

My Prayer Request...

_____

_____

_____

_____

_____

_____

_____

_____

_____

_____

_____

_____

_____

_____

_____

_____

_____

_____

_____

_____

_____

Hear My Prayer"

Prayer Request For Others...

_____

_____

_____

_____

_____

_____

_____

_____

_____

_____

_____

Answered Prayers

_____

_____

_____

_____

_____

_____

"Dear Lord,

Date: _____

My Prayer Request...

_____

_____

_____

_____

_____

_____

_____

_____

_____

_____

_____

_____

_____

_____

_____

_____

_____

_____

_____

_____

_____

_____

Hear My Prayer"

Prayer Request For Others...

_____
_____
_____
_____
_____
_____
_____
_____
_____
_____
_____
_____
_____

Answered Prayers

_____
_____
_____
_____
_____
_____

"Dear Lord,

Date: _____

My Prayer Request...

_____

_____

_____

_____

_____

_____

_____

_____

_____

_____

_____

_____

_____

_____

_____

_____

_____

_____

_____

_____

_____

_____

Hear My Prayer"

Prayer Request For Others...

_____

_____

_____

_____

_____

_____

_____

_____

_____

_____

_____

_____

Answered Prayers

_____

_____

_____

_____

_____

_____

"Dear Lord,

Date: _____

My Prayer Request...

_____

_____

_____

_____

_____

_____

_____

_____

_____

_____

_____

_____

_____

_____

_____

_____

_____

_____

_____

_____

_____

Hear My Prayer"

Prayer Request For Others...

_____

_____

_____

_____

_____

_____

_____

_____

_____

_____

_____

_____

Answered Prayers

_____

_____

_____

_____

_____

"Dear Lord,

Date: _____

My Prayer Request...

_____

_____

_____

_____

_____

_____

_____

_____

_____

_____

_____

_____

_____

_____

_____

_____

_____

_____

_____

_____

_____

_____

Hear My Prayer″

Prayer Request For Others...

_____

_____

_____

_____

_____

_____

_____

_____

_____

_____

_____

_____

<u>Answered Prayers</u>

_____

_____

_____

_____

_____

"Dear Lord,

Date: _____

My Prayer Request...

_____

_____

_____

_____

_____

_____

_____

_____

_____

_____

_____

_____

_____

_____

_____

_____

_____

_____

_____

_____

_____

_____

Hear My Prayer"

Prayer Request For Others...

_____
_____
_____
_____
_____
_____
_____
_____
_____
_____
_____
_____
_____

Answered Prayers

_____
_____
_____
_____
_____
_____

"Dear Lord,

Date: _____

My Prayer Request...

_____

_____

_____

_____

_____

_____

_____

_____

_____

_____

_____

_____

_____

_____

_____

_____

_____

_____

_____

_____

Hear My Prayer"

Prayer Request For Others...

_____

_____

_____

_____

_____

_____

_____

_____

_____

_____

_____

_____

_____

<u>Answered Prayers</u>

_____

_____

_____

_____

_____

"Rejoice always, pray continually, give thanks in all circumstances; for this is God's will for you in Christ Jesus."

1 Thessalonians 5:16 - 18

"Dear Lord,

Date: _____

My Prayer Request...

_____

_____

_____

_____

_____

_____

_____

_____

_____

_____

_____

_____

_____

_____

_____

_____

_____

_____

_____

Hear My Prayer"

Prayer Request For Others...

_____

_____

_____

_____

_____

_____

_____

_____

_____

_____

_____

_____

_____

Answered Prayers

_____

_____

_____

_____

_____

"Dear Lord,

Date: _____

My Prayer Request...

_____

_____

_____

_____

_____

_____

_____

_____

_____

_____

_____

_____

_____

_____

_____

_____

_____

_____

_____

_____

_____

_____

Hear My Prayer"

Prayer Request For Others...

_____

_____

_____

_____

_____

_____

_____

_____

_____

_____

_____

_____

Answered Prayers

_____

_____

_____

_____

_____

_____

"Dear Lord,

Date: _____

My Prayer Request...

_____

_____

_____

_____

_____

_____

_____

_____

_____

_____

_____

_____

_____

_____

_____

_____

_____

_____

_____

_____

_____

_____

_____

Hear My Prayer"

Prayer Request For Others...

_____

_____

_____

_____

_____

_____

_____

_____

_____

_____

_____

_____

_____

<u>Answered Prayers</u>

_____

_____

_____

_____

_____

_____

"Dear Lord,

Date: _____

My Prayer Request...

_____

_____

_____

_____

_____

_____

_____

_____

_____

_____

_____

_____

_____

_____

_____

_____

_____

_____

_____

Hear My Prayer"

Prayer Request For Others...

_____

_____

_____

_____

_____

_____

_____

_____

_____

_____

_____

_____

_____

<u>Answered Prayers</u>

_____

_____

_____

_____

_____

"Dear Lord,

Date: _____

My Prayer Request...

_____

_____

_____

_____

_____

_____

_____

_____

_____

_____

_____

_____

_____

_____

_____

_____

_____

_____

_____

_____

_____

Hear My Prayer"

Prayer Request For Others...

_____

_____

_____

_____

_____

_____

_____

_____

_____

_____

_____

_____

<u>Answered Prayers</u>

_____

_____

_____

_____

_____

"Dear Lord,

Date: _____

My Prayer Request...

_____

_____

_____

_____

_____

_____

_____

_____

_____

_____

_____

_____

_____

_____

_____

_____

_____

_____

_____

_____

_____

Hear My Prayer"

Prayer Request For Others...

_____

_____

_____

_____

_____

_____

_____

_____

_____

_____

_____

_____

Answered Prayers

_____

_____

_____

_____

_____

"Dear Lord,

Date: _____

My Prayer Request...

_____

_____

_____

_____

_____

_____

_____

_____

_____

_____

_____

_____

_____

_____

_____

_____

_____

_____

_____

_____

_____

_____

_____

_____

Hear My Prayer"

Prayer Request For Others...

_____

_____

_____

_____

_____

_____

_____

_____

_____

_____

_____

_____

_____

<u>Answered Prayers</u>

_____

_____

_____

_____

_____

"If you believe, you will receive whatever you ask for in prayer."

Matthew 21:22

CPSIA information can be obtained
at www.ICGtesting.com
Printed in the USA
LVHW020312140920
665930LV00019B/685